On The Stand

On The Stand

Américo Casiano Jr.

iUniverse, Inc.
New York Lincoln Shanghai

On The Stand

Copyright © 2007 by Américo Casiano Jr.

All rights reserved. No part of this book may be used or reproduced by any means, graphic, electronic, or mechanical, including photocopying, recording, taping or by any information storage retrieval system without the written permission of the publisher except in the case of brief quotations embodied in critical articles and reviews.

iUniverse books may be ordered through booksellers or by contacting:

iUniverse
2021 Pine Lake Road, Suite 100
Lincoln, NE 68512
www.iuniverse.com
1-800-Authors (1-800-288-4677)

Because of the dynamic nature of the Internet, any Web addresses or links contained in this book may have changed since publication and may no longer be valid.

The views expressed in this work are solely those of the author and do not necessarily reflect the views of the publisher, and the publisher hereby disclaims any responsibility for them.
This book was printed via the international internet online publishing agreements and systems; all international ownership rights—intellectual property rights, copyrights, and other rights defined by all international law, interstate, and international commerce and trade agreements, treaties current, and perpetual belong to the author.
First Edition

ISBN: 978-0-595-43289-9 (pbk)
ISBN: 978-0-595-87630-3 (ebk)

Printed in the United States of America

The following poems have been published in various literary magazines, journals, and/or anthologies:

Tonight by Vendor's Booth. *Aloud: Voices from the Nuyorican Poets' Café. M. Algarin et al. New York: Holt/Owl. 1993.*

For Michael S. Harper. *The Next World: Poems by Third World Americans. J. Bruchac III. Trumansburg: Crossing Press. 1976.*

Salicrup. *Aloud: Voices from the Nuyorican Poets' Café. M. Algarin et al. New York: Holt/Owl. 1993.*

Para Juaco A Message in Two Languages. *The Next World: Poems by Third World Americans. J. Bruchac III. Trumansburg: Crossing Press. 1976.*

Car Six. *New Rain Volume 9: Our Fathers/Ourselves. Gary Johnston et al. New York: Blind Beggar Press. 1999.*

Puente. *Bum Rush the Page: Def Poetry Jam. T. Medina et al. New York: Crown Publishing. 2001.*

Casiano's Mission: Quisqueya Earth Probe. *New Rain Volume 9: Our Fathers/Ourselves. Gary Johnston et al. New York: Blind Beggar Press. 1999.*

The author would like to thank Mr. Ted Berger, executive director and Ms. Aimee Lee, program officer-grants of the New York Foundation for the Arts for their support, as well as Mr. Bill Aguado, executive director of the Bronx Council on the Arts.

Contents

Foreword... xi
Introduction... xiii
My People... 1
- *maturation*.. 2
- *music box*... 3
- *tonight by vendor's booth*............................. 4
- *Sixta*... 5
- *Lares: earthly inspiration: oration for Coca*.......... 6
- *Polito*.. 7
- *poetry as cosmic: El Batey*............................ 8
- *afroboricuaism*.. 9
- *my people*.. 10
- *9/11/01: ode to family: requiem for your soul*........ 11

Poem for My Subconscious................................. 13
- *poem for my subconscious*............................. 14
- *(untitled)*... 15
- *garrison*... 16
- *one twenty one*....................................... 17
- *for Michael S. Harper*................................ 18
- *prayer*... 19

Institute of Some Kind of Studies........................ 21
- *Institute of Some Kind of Studies*.................... 22
- *Salicrup*... 23
- *obese mode   purity is obsession*..................... 25
- *Saratoga Springs*..................................... 26

- *para Juaco a message in two languages* 27
- *3:02* 29

On the Stand 31
- *car six* 32
- *three two* 33
- *halse* 35
- *ode to bronx river* 37
- *Libre* 39
- *a night in tunisia* 40
- *poem for Dr. Tone* 41
- *Puente* 43
- *Toque El Taller* 44
- *Toque Mayo* 45
- *Toque Siete* 46
- *Toque Ocha* 47
- *sax* 48
- *second meditations* 49

Afterthought 51
- *pues ya que te fuiste* 52
- *Casiano's mission: Quisqueya earth probe: nena* 53
- *ode to el beso negro* 54
- *sunset* 55
- *blue mountain lake* 56
- *afterthought* 57

Glossary of Terms 59
Artistic Biography 65

To Américo Casiano Cruz, my dad, for teaching me honor. May he rest in peace.
To Sixta Lugo, my mother, for giving me endless love and teaching me perseverance, faith, and hope.
To Norberto Casiano and his wife, Hilda, my godparents.
To my uncle and aunts, Martiñano, Pasquala, Maria, Florentina, Leonide.
To my cousins Santa Alonzo Casiano and her husband Edwin; Judy and her husband Frank; Tony Velez and his wife Nilsa; and Armatina and Gloria, for being my heroes.

Foreword

I was introduced to Américo Casiano Jr. by a blank sheet of paper during the first meeting of my fiction course at Brooklyn College in February 1972. I began the class by asking, "What is literature?" Various opinions were tentatively offered and mulled over. Finally, we moved into "art for art's sake" vs. "everything is political." The guy who seemed to have opinions on everything argued as the class stared vacantly at the ripped notebook page he thrust into the air. "What?" "Like I said, apples that chair, clothes, anything. Anything that is *is* political! Even this sheet of paper!" I jabbered about a lack of message, about defining words within an appropriate context (to no avail). The page quavered adamantly, and I sensed that it should be reported to the proper publishers.

Meanwhile, friendship intervened. Being poets, we both grew to distrust constricting definitions. Nevertheless, I am happy to say that in this foreword to his poetry, I finally have my chance to make some sense of Américo's page.

Like his contemporaries Victor Hernandez Cruz, Pedro Juan Pietri, and Sandra Maria Esteves, Américo Casiano Jr. is the voice of a people straddling two worlds. The past and the future are migrations. Caribbean sun, tongues, drum, earth, the ancestral soulscapes of Puerto Rico—all of these pervade Casiano's poems. Home is reminiscence and return, a spiritual journey along *Joyuda* and the road running past cane fields near his birthplace in Cabo Rojo, where his father stands in the night near his vendor's booth. There are other voyages through mean streets to where a friend lies on a tenement roof in the South Bronx, "sailing back" to a junkie's nowhere island.

The perspective of the survivor informs most of his poems, particularly "Para Juaco." But that perspective is blurred by subtle complexities, for Casiano's poetry, though often addressed to others (friend or alien), is essentially meditative. The poems are dialogues of the self: playful, tough-spirited, ironic, sentimental, urbane, and raw. Some are private, sifting words into elliptical, imagistic patterns like lyrical puzzles in which the reader is the missing piece. In other poems, Casiano assumes the role of communal poet—forthright, rhetorical, and impassioned. Casiano "gives key" through his commitment to uplifting those floundering in negativism, intra-racial prejudice, and political and economic contradiction.

Many Third World poets have significantly contributed toward defining positive goals in their peoples' struggle for liberation. Américo Casiano's talent enhances that legacy. Welcome to mi hermano—printed pages and all.

Charles Lynch, Brooklyn, New York

Introduction

The political upheaval of the late 1960s galvanized a generation of New York Puerto Ricans, both culturally and politically. For these young Puerto Ricans, the 1960s were a time when they were moving in two directions at once—on the one hand, searching for their roots and history, and on the other, determining their direction for the future. This dynamic was reflected in their culture—for example music and poetry—and developments in the cultural sphere, in turn, nurtured the political movements. Américo Casiano's verse eloquently captures and reflects this dynamic.

In the 1960s, progressive-thinking composers and authors introduced new sounds and words that signaled the emergence of a tough urban voice that appealed to both Puerto Ricans and African-Americans.

This contemporary urban voice fused rhythm and a cosmopolitan imagery with language—at times two languages—and became popular with young Puerto Ricans and African-Americans. It offered a cultural bridge between the two communities that mirrored the political sphere, where the Young Lords and the Black Panthers were insisting that Puerto Rican and African-American unity was a prerequisite for progressive change. Many premiere artists were able to stretch beyond the limits of their respective formats and develop fine work.

Dynamic developments like the Puerto Rican/Latino and African-American collaborations of the forties, fifties, sixties, and seventies represented a healthy cross-fertilization and the cultural milieu of these artists who were reaching out to their traditional roots while at the same time creating their respective art. The blending of roots and histories as well as the blending of artistic formats has to be appreciated as a natural occurrence in American reality—that is, a dynamic phenomenon in Western multi-racial society. Artists influenced by popular communal events or movements produced works that speak for and inspire those events or movements.

The energy generated by the community struggles was supported and inspired by Américo Casiano Jr. and other contemporaries like Jesus Papoleto Melendez, Pedro Juan Pietri, and Sandra Maria Esteves, among, others, who were raised within this cultural environment. This work of this generation of word masters differed from the poetry emanating from Puerto Rico in terms of language, style, format, and point of view. Their works reflected the duality experienced by *Boricuas* in the United States. It is another expression of the simultaneous movement towards roots and toward the future.

Some of our creative artists got trapped in a repetitive cycle, fixating on a single aspect of our reality and exploring it over and over until they hit a dead end, collapsing, exhausted, like dogs chasing their tails. Often the fixation was on street life, drugs, and prison.

Américo Casiano Jr., however, is able to transcend the one-dimensional, limited focus and explore the complexity and variety of our lives—our past and our future, our desires and our demons. Read Américo's work carefully. It reflects community life, the fight against the drug scourge, the experiences of driving a livery cab in New York, and the struggle for justice. His work celebrates the beauty of who we are—a multi-racial, multi-skilled community of working people.

Two additional aspects of Américo's work, I think, deserve attention. The first is his willingness to share with us the quest for family reconciliation. He explores the way in which we may come to terms with both the contradiction within *la familia* as well as pay homage to those elders who paved the way.

The second is Américo's love for and tribute to the musical geniuses who emerged from our midst, and to the musical masters who laid the foundation. In verse that hums, percolates, and bops, he reminds us of how music and poetry feed our spirits and make us strong.

I began this piece by talking about the explosion of the 1960s because I met Américo when we were both members of the Young Lords working out of the Bronx office on Longwood Avenue, and because his poetry reminds me of the dynamic move in two directions at once.

The necessity of moving in two directions at once—to our roots and to our future—confuses some people, but it makes other people deep, more appreciative of the complexities of life and the joy of living.

Richard Perez
New York City

My People

maturation

born from a womb fixed eighteen degrees north of the equator
I was mistaken for a *crazy* woman's child
mother laughed as she told the tale
we migrated on my fortieth day

across the Atlantic we stage-coached
peeping through clouds
huge apple conditions   horse gallops
mind is cold turkey
I gobble words
the militant obscenities vomit
buttons on an applejack
wet pavement   wheelchair   Beirut
the automatic weapon

children unload like calves at a rail yard
they run into cottages doors closing behind them steam
the bathroom tiles scream sodomy

graffiti rapes the hallways   the dim lights offer silhouette
the counselor screws   the violet ones attack the night watchman
night playing hush song of darkness   grass burning fingertips
jazz

music box

I arrived at Mani
translation peanut

driving through Lares
movement slows the music box sings

mama 'buela
mama 'buela

here stands the Aquarian
bringing rain to mountain of coffee
Joyuda
chorus of the sea
makes you lay iron on ground
shame on those who deny their brownness

mama 'buela
mama 'buela

here
island lays
waiting to swing
night comes we drink two bars
El Cóqui continues to sing

I will always praise those mired
in the earth
don't worry if you are defined by the sun
soon I'll give you key

just lay low fake a purr

tonight by vendor's booth

drums make legs jump
hair glow like night
in Cabo Rojo tumba plays
mosquitoes buzz among mango leaves
wind crossing the fruitless tree
twilight creeps through my father's eyes
tart like the quenepas on the old tree
they have sprinkled salt on his hair
added half a keg to his waste

mellowing
I pilgrim here
to moon with him
along quiet road spirit sulky
along the shore

Sixta

Sixta of La Garita
of a home eaten by bees
I know you as powdery sand
beaten by waves
inhaling exhaling
shell fish walking the Bronx
face hunched
he is poet of yard bird mode

and you are another
withering in a stain frozen room
toiling cleaning the toilet of my playground

and as I write the poem of your coffee
I will call you mother
mulched in Puerto Rico
where you made me in the image
of my father

hinging to your menopause
hands bosoming your grandchildren's smile

and that yearning to return

Lares: earthly inspiration: oration for Coca

for Santa Alonzo Casiano

grainy gingerbread
breathing like an earth toad
thickset along the gritty road
creeping slowly across Edwin's
oatmeal eyes

your caverns echo phoneme
carved into the bark of your coffee
peaking within the woven leaves
branches and morning haze

in the distance the murmuring roosters
bobbing to a bolero

arms and legs cut the mist hands pulling
feet pushing blade pruning
your rhythmic hand on the washboard
accompanying pandera and tambourine

on the cassette
an improvised song of jealous knife
and revenging pistol

Lares
cup of my syllables
the anarchist speaks of you

as a rifle in the hills
but within the foliage of this mountainous
countryside

it is only Coca tending kitchen
Boricua sofrito sizzling in the skillet.

Polito

glum face of La Garita
globetrotting corners
searching for definition

rooster croaks three times
and you are the forsaken

never were you fed love pabulum
or told of your sire

in your dawn I betrayed you
drove first stake into your arm's valley
in your name and in the name of others

now you stand dancing
on a cross

poetry as cosmic: El Batey

I arrived at the village
along its narrow streets
pale hair   acidy mind

headlights move along the wall
night speaking bohemia

I enter El Batey
cosmic as the counterpoints
mimicking a Yoruba dance
Laviera becomes Olú

tongue savoring lower eastside
he speaks his id

syntax praising the drum
we are brushes

packing the mud

afroboricuaism

for Richard David and Charles Oscar Moore

once
the clouds stopped crying
the sun
became a native son
to the earth
later they married
gave birth to stars
that made the milky way

my people

don't
tell me
color
doesn't
bother
you

    when
    black
    is
    mentioned
    you
    grind
    your
    teeth

        if
        you
        aren't
        careful
        some
        might
        paint
        your neck
        red

9/11/01: ode to family: requiem for your soul

for Tony Velez, his son and daughter

why did I move up
beyond the Cloisters?
I should have been spawned in the water, air, and fire
that caught and buried your friends:

Alexander Ortiz,
directing hundreds of people
out of tower one
only to go back in and never return.

Ramon Grijalvo,
quiet, soft-spoken, teaching himself
programming languages
while piles of paper and coffee cups
lined his cubicle
because he too wanted
to excel in the IT department.

among the muddy streets
the love of dead fathers, invisible, perpetual
if not in fire, in air,
lingers
raping the innocence of a moment's calm

as a rubber doll fails to squeak
when stepped on; obliterated by fireballs,
wrenched screams, smashed heads,
and milk spilled over.

in this charred valley
you are cheek, painful heels,
shinbones, and gullet
feeding contentedly.

so, let me lament
with you and friends
admiring you for yelling
into your walkie-talkie
"Angeeeel!
It's your father, answer, answer me;
I'm looking for you; I'm all right!"

the silence on the walkie-talkie
deafening.

the site dark, soot-laden,
dirt-filled,
attacked by misguided pride.

but soul and contemplation
inspire us to search
for your son;
for our universal and immortal
values raised like battlefield tents
above your daughter
crouched in a slimy corner
of a subway station

crying
yet remembering
that mothers and fathers
sowed the seeds among these metal thorns
that explode and burn
worn-out bodies that hunger for life
and signs of new light.

Poem for My Subconscious

poem for my subconscious

many men have glared at your pain
they watch you in rigor mortis
stiffing the stroll

and as police glaze your stallion turned stable
you live in hallways grizzled by that flour

see the street juice back its history
remember the fifties? Our elders jumping salty
'cause your knobs were buckling
o Jodie your song is blues
like Red Garland's fingers dancing
on the main drag of many tears your spirit howls

look towards that Stormville in Greenhaven
Julio is you   now they call you sender
shiv inspiring excitement
and when Shepp blows change
in a wheelchair we come
to write another chapter: Attica

(untitled)

it all began in the Old San Juan
as if to be a motion picture men sit
discerning the esoteric dancer

like an erotic dance machine
legs dangle above their heads
movement speaking lustfully

all are mute taking dictation

garrison

tonight I saw a string of green pearls
strung along your width
everything went one way

ligature
one breath of multi-blue
curling along Hunts Point
held in a black hand driving
tractor grinding gears
lost in change

lifework
renovated rubble
cascara piano
that Spanish guitar strung
Rhumba Son

inanimate object
a bushel of ghetto weed

And that always present rustling

one twenty one

it's annoying
beginning a voyage
on an old "Stand By Me" melody

since
what fuels is breath
grunts exhaling furnace
mooring
entertaining morpheme
sense and structure

beyond that
a churning wheel
rutty pavement   oil slick exit

for Michael S. Harper

standing alone in a corner
I heard you singing of a Bird living dead
and I remember one afternoon
a brother laid on a rooftop
in a pool of urine alone
eyes closed   sailing back

prayer

for Louis "Boogie" Corasco

farewell
don't be angry
those who shot didn't know
when you meet again
look straight into their eyes and explain

those who were dancing
before
on a roof were you

but you changed
the one who shot didn't know
don't be angry

just come back
tell your son not to worry

for you still live in trees
birds in flight

Institute of Some Kind of Studies

**institute of
some kind of studies
somewhere college
of some place
somewhere, some place
telephone: (&!*) *^%#&%!**

For Dr. Alfredo Matilla

I looked today/at night
toilet flushed/Apocalipsis

coffee grinds/your mind
top secret/you're a hoe

PhD listens/to a fart
in chaos

and upon crossing the river
fishes pollute the air

Salicrup

for Fernando Salicrup

at the cellar of your imagination
hatchet hand about to chop rooster's neck
coiling cognition   pheasant's crest
phallic in profile it leans long
'til Adam apples huge breast
picturing a womb its lips hair a woman
body oval tits join rooster's wing
again hard-curving lines
again the phallic head
the prick like nose of El Píchon
abstraction   Buddha   the hanging tits
eyes   composition
the tight angles running
perpendicular to an African mask

eyes shadow the tiger
it is the soul of your conscience
thought thighs your brother about to mine a canon
cocaine   pussy   leg   suit
A shirt and tie   claws floor other organic growth
the boyish butterflies flutter
are they the real free creatures?
hen gobbling water   *pechuga*   skeleton
all is ass and hinting Old San Juan
anal hairs   another face   legs   foot
a vulture's beak
between the legs of this awkward hen
a seed stems about to flower

beyond your imagination
bridges slope Manhattan
sheet metal rusts and corrodes the river
pillars wade   reflection   a neon city

On The Stand

the east river curves   the bridge splits
the avenue turns into figures
the court jester juggles his balls
the impossible one smokes pot
the bricks plain like buildings downed by arson
the shrubs brown as urine waters its roots
traffic stalls   it blurs the morning
hellgate pier   the bleating river   creation

it's the green grime along Harlem's riverbanks
the fungi seeping old schools
raping our children candy stores rack up their shelves
billiards eight-ball Hispanics   Christmas   hailing snow

a bed sheet on the ground

obese mode   purity is obsession

you came on stage modeling the strings of your mother
the Danzón of your complexion enticing high mode
I heard your soft melodies
enrich the acoustics of Avery
and we were there with Charlie on his scales obese with funk
In one mode   in a single oneness
one to one   in modality

and Cachao take me back to your obsession
the night laden with stars above your hands slapping   Cuba

Saratoga Springs

I arrived on the last quarter moon
as the sky sits overcast
and Saturn rises behind Venus
and high tide hugs the shoreline
of the Long Island Sound
like a tenor saxophone
crooning for color and texture

I yearn for firm breasts
as brown as the drinking water of Baghdad

Teddy Edwards lays in wake
deft to the ligature and McGhee's
trumpet caught in Mars and Jupiter's melody
French kissing the dry banks
of East LA

Dominican parents wait
for the casket of their son
as Spas sit empty
like the nests of Mallards
located on tall old pine branches

as pilot whales run aground
and navy bombs pollute Vieques' shoreline
a sister mulls over the taste of cold pancakes
smothered with frozen strawberries

wondering
If whites gets the same treatment

para Juaco a message in two languages

        los ojos te miran
        entiende, mi hermano

los ojos te miran
como las aguas naturales del rió Harlem
ellos hablan un poema del sol
y usted es el sol

        pero te digo, hermano
        los ojos te miran

you a vibrating tumbao
in an ivy league suit
a dos golpes going wild
can you hear them?—they play your song

        pero, brother
        te digo otra ves
        que los ojos te miran

the moon danced buffalo spirits
in the nude 'cause you,
a fine edged machete,
Like panther is your nickname,
You wait to pounce on your prey

and I tell you, brother,
los ojos te siguen mirando

como los traffic lights miran al antillano
en Nueva York
empujándole agujas en los brazos
y al mismo tiempo cambiándose
La cara

the room fills with jealous vibrations
Brooklyn College gives a bulletin
General Information:
      aquí tienes dos panitas
      Laviera Casiano
      Casiano Laviera
      dos puños del Caribe
      Casiano el mar
      Laviera la tierra

juntos en El yoismos
apoyan tu posición

¿pues y que de los ojos?
esos ojos blanco llamados riot squad
esos ojos que se quillan de ser blanco ...
si a eso ojos
que tiran balas de racismo
      bochinches
      y elloismos

y que matan niños de dieciséis años
a esos ojos
nosotros le diremos
que el verdadero Boricua

es solamente ¡fuego!

3:02

continuing
I peek past chibos and grunt

the folding cot has given me
my finer moments

i seek comfort in the mermaid
offering white and red flowers

my own claim to mountain earth
and ore

On the Stand

car six

snow falls
like frozen fish scale
the jagged Hudson runs
as if it were blood
from a bullet hole

you wake up
feeling the surgeon's pull
fear lingering
nightmare: tarry shadows

that old Colombian coronel
the three wives of Leo

like a plastic bag
they cling to your intestine
and suck out your waist

spotlight:
that old Peruvian Eva
giving you lustful stares

morpheme: you nibbling her tit

three two

gripping your mic you mumbled
your raspy voice sending Sarge into a rage
red boil erupting his neck Irish volcano

i remember Gaddy riding shotgun
wooing our women on Bainbridge
painting across Bronx walls china doll
the many faces of Tashitu

and in a dark gas station
Your chocolate hand gripping
a twenty-five
Gut tight ready to fire
black rose wiggling her stiff ass
jealous of your desire
other white women

sadness is you
missing toe path and heartbeat
found beneath wrinkled mint
'trane dipping memory Africa
clean pores and

"… if you wanna be my baby,
woman, you can't run around
cause if you gonna run around,
you can put my money down …"

but back to your godfather
sun standing in wake

On The Stand

like a leaf of an African violet
your ears dance in green
Allen mimicking your Bojangles
singing H-A-DOUBLE-R-I-G-A-N
spells Harry
of the Blue White checker cabs
of a brotherhood found on rutty parkways
paving our sleepless nights
cold steel pressing against our necks
feeling the chill of precise commands
numb cheek feeling cold coarse ground
distance
is Jerry's trumpet improvising
Lover Man

halse

cantaloupe casaba and honeydew
cannot compare with your melony voice

held in its hand
night spreads it across Parkchester's
Soundview cloud ridge a black sand star
hulking out receding hairline
holding it in a mangrove
of looming muggers
melodiously shouting
faces weary and beaten
like a Colombian held up in a railcar
sister lying dead
post mortem decomposing dream
fed with breast
young pearl eyes
looming in the dark

again we mingle on the stand
clave being quick nine
and inquiry into whose high booker
road jocks raving over their glom
hidden within their humor

and Halse
it be Fleming's way
twice held up in the dark Commons
blunt blade tucked under his neck
command edging into his ear
clinging to his nervous sweat
throat scraped red

melpomene:
his long wrinkled fingers raking his bowed Afro
the Jamaican Eskimo staring down
stick-up man hawking the Circle
as a black mother maintains
her bedside vigil

heartbeat riding her James' gypsy cab

ode to bronx river

the snake plant
reminds me of grandfather
and long walks beneath willow trees
along the Wec-quaes-qeek riverbank
where wigwams and longhouse lodged wampum and Sachem
cautious of Sewanakie—the salt-water people

Sawanakie came in his long boat
from the easy-flowing river
came out of fogbank
near where the rivers meet
where Sachem and Wappingos approached
curious of these new salt-water men

the bearded one whispered,
"Durst not trust them"
and thunder bellowed from their weapons
arrows heaved in response
near the shoreline of the "Bronck"

and one Sawanakie slumps still
two others in crimson heap

I reflect back beyond the retreat
their nation killed by smallpox and malaria
and the war of 1643

and gone are the villages of Alipconk,
Wysquaqua, and Rechtuak
and gone are the wampum
of black clamshells
and freshly grown corn, bean, and squash
and potato roasted in campfires
and the snake plant
reminds me of grandfather
and lone walks beneath willow trees
and wine bottles and broken things
that no one breaks

but were broken nevertheless.

Libre

for Manny Oquendo

you need not dive into oil
sweat makes you slick

beneath night spread and feathered
stars pave silence

my mother's kitten walks in heat
young males purr against bar
full moon turning crescent
numb shadows catching the bends

along Westchester Avenue rustic barrels
flame   rotten food
exhaust fumes   crackling hands

your fingers slap and muff the bongo skin
giving homage to your deity and those before you
pupils squinting   sparks painting somber image
pushing through your arms
alternating current flowing infinite   free   in clave

a night in tunisia

for Andy Gonzalez

a radiator valve slowly whistles.
the steam floating
across the air conditioner's face.

the baby bass rises from its slant
its fingers pluck the sound of raindrops
where the landfill fails to stop the floods
or a pair of thin sticks smacking
against a metal edge.

again your fingers syncopate
along the worn ebony neck
sulky beneath an overcast sky.

everyone gathers around your parlor
cluttered with ancient recordings
of impeccable clave.

tokes and cough continuing,
piss running red.

poem for Dr. Tone

for Kenny Kirkland

imagine a drummer
playing a Cuban cascara rhythm
on a worn wooden floor
in a Dominican restaurant
on Dykeman Street and Broadway

imagine two Timbales sticks
playing an accompanying rhythm on cowbells
and two humongous hands slapping
and syncopating on five congas
while their shirtsleeves flutter
rhythmically unbuttoned but in clave

imagine a baby bass
held firmly plucked with precision
the bass line an old bebop standard
cranked up to a Cuban two/three beat
the trumpet player a black Cuban
with a Moorish smile
careful ladies, if he catches your ear
he'll convince you he's from Andalusia

the young man
with the copper skin and a gentleman's cane
limps to the stage making his way
to the fender piano

his smile his keyboard playing
the "Blue Turtles' Dream" and the dreams
of his Puerto Rican mother
massaging his sore leg

renowned   world-traveled
walking in the footsteps of Tizol's "Caravan"
down a "Parisian Thoroughfare"
looking for "Don Quixote"

his fingers exhibiting
the "Tonality of Atonement"
and 'Tain knows and knows why
his heartbeat will always play
in the graveyards of our soul.

Puente

let's not talk of the subway series
or dead birds or mosquitoes
or robust crops of pollen

let's not talk of air raids
or naval assaults eroding Vieques
we both know the fish will not return
to feed the curb of hungry stomachs

the stalking barracuda is oblivious to our pain
so let's not frown or slip into moods
when the empty spotlight appears on the bandstand
where he stood, face brimming with that enigmatic grin
navigating him through the business
the cosmos welcomes him
as we file past his coffin

it is my understanding,
according to the flute player,

that all he sought out of life was a
standing ovation.

Toque El Taller

for Tito Martin y Jorge Soto

hands slapping dead flesh force
blood and sweat pour into psalms
and Maceo is reborn stomping

bloods
don't bring out the calumet
'til the last drum is silent

remember all fingers point to the land

Toque Mayo

now that the April rain is gone
and the human gnomes
appear again

life
becomes an endeavor

Toque Siete

these canoes these shrubs these totems scattered
are the remains of centuries toughened by dry dust
empty like the promises made
these masks portray sullen sea earth
and dead sun hanging twilight
on its long peak pointing south
toward my mother

these drums
repetitious resonance beating

remind me of Ife gourd rattling Diablito
walking corridors

flute continuing in the background
straw skin deities

we move toward sunset.

Toque Ocha

Vicente, Gene, y Milton
omojuba elegba eshu
oshosi shango

o'mbatala

sax

for Mario Rivera

the gig is over
what bangs on you is soft morning
its fingers walk in Spanish chords
courting sunrise

the clatter angers Sucia
Junior watches from the sink
the notes curl from your chalice
burning trembling

into oblivion

second meditations

for Steve Turre

so what if no one understands
you were born to speak through quiet eyes
rough-edged rock spirit
the glitter of your long, braided hair

it is your breath sustaining whole note
blown through conch shells
your daughter's eyes

confirmation love aché
the endless dripping of
a faucet

Afterthought

pues ya que te fuiste

I'll speak of quiet things
the lull on the Deegan
the swaying of mini-blinds
raising hairline
soft pinch of lips
tasting like gingerbread
mints
and perfumed subsoil

summit
raises and levels in nine month intervals

like passionate hounds, we sniff for new beginnings

Casiano's mission: Quisqueya earth probe: nena

I persist with my own grace
and thirst to shift from equity to subservience.
I mine, drink from pungent, mossy riverbed
daring those others to call you profane cow.

breaking dawn
we spread eagle,
offer murmuring of waves
breaking twilight.

like a snail creeping slowly
across your winded mouth,
I sling tadpoles and milky pods
anchoring your fields of wheat.

my kisses
gracefully calming
the weariness and aches that come after.

ode to el beso negro

once again, you return
gnawing my neck like an ingrown hair
pulling me beyond the curled grass
to where the rump spreads the dry mud.

I sniff,
sampling the wrinkles smeared
like bumpy cracks.

again the scent
the anxious twitch and pull of Venus
and Jupiter riding high moon
swelling like the high tide of salty rivers.

our lust
eagerly making you forget
the stress and pressure of patriarch
and Christian mother betrayed
by electroshocks, immigrant scams,
and adulterous affairs living an edgy existence
behind us
the steel-landscaped window,
polansky's lithograph illustrating *The Call*,
the African batik hanging on the wall.

we close our eyes.
behind us
the widow with her egocentric moods
yelling and screaming incessantly
complaining of loud humming
and electric drilling

y otra ves
deseamos ser perros.

sunset

even when it rains
the gray curtain fails to obscure
each smoldering gleam
each reddish amber
hiding your shy eyes

you veil
the incandescent lamp

disrobe
your eyelids

I clasp
your rump tight
as I hear my name

whispered
as if it were a defiant secret

repeated
as if hexed by innocence
flung out of control

after the storm
we bathe
and
drink from the bedrock

like Olympic skiers running the slalom
we ski down slope
feeling the frigid stiffness of peaks and timber

Venus leaving us with Uranus
Jupiter standing guard

Neptune ebbing along the Sound.

blue mountain lake

you sit at the foot of the mountain
dominating the landscape
lulling the blue-green slopes
subdued like leaning branches
of White Ash.

their shadow lingers above
my sweaty forehead
like a Loon bobbing in sweet water
waiting to dive for food

gone are the famed eagles
nesting in that tree overlooking the bay
and mountain trails leading to your peak

below
your fifteen sisters

gone are the miners digging
deep within those rugged scares feeding
black bears, ospreys, and Stillwater

I seek the Smallmouth Bass
the Bull Moose looming within a mist
where the beavers pack the mud

near the canal
where the headless Eva
haunts
the hallways
of her husband's mansion

gliding
like a hue at sunrise.

afterthought

and like the quicksilver
my breath hastens
as I climb the hill
huffing and puffing visions of old Indians

I watch pirates steal land
lap your streams with my tongue

suspended
in sound of rivers and waterfalls

Glossary of Terms

Batey—In the indigenous Arawak culture, the Batey was a dwelling hut made of wood and bamboo. During the 1970s, El Batey was the name of a café located on McDougal Street in the Greenwich Village neighborhood of New York City that was popularized by Puerto Ricans and other Latinos.

Boricua—The popular name for Puerto Ricans. It was derived from the indigenous Arawak word: Boriken.

Bronck—A reference to John Bronck, for whom the borough of the Bronx is named. Bronck settled on the lower coastline of the Bronx around the area know as Mott Haven.

Cachao—Israel "Cachao" Lopez, Cuban composer, bassist, and band leader. Cachao was instrumental in the innovation and evolution of Afro-Cuban music. Cachao incorporated into his style of playing the rhythmic slapping associated with the conga drum alluded to in the last stanza.

Charlie—A reference to Puerto Rican pianist Charlie Palmieri, older brother of Eddie Palmieri. Charlie played with many of the Afro-Cuban dance bands of the 1940s, 1950s, and 1960s.

Chibo—In the Puerto Rican common vernacular when one is painting an apartment or a room and misses a spot it is referred to as "un chibo."

Cóqui (or Kóki)—The family nickname for the author.

Danzón—A type of Cuban music that is the official music of Cuba, derived from European-influenced ballroom dance developed in the second half of the 19th century. The precursors of Danzón are the *contradanza*, *Danza* and the *habanera* music, all of which have their roots in French music, which in turn was influenced by German and Italian music that arrived in Cuba via Haiti. To read more see http://en.wikipedia.org/wiki/Danzon.

Don Quixote—A composition written by Milton Nascimento and Antonio Cesar Camargo Mariano and arranged by Kenny Kirkland for Charles Fambrough, The Proper Angle, CTI Records, 1991.

Dr. Tone—The nickname of pianist, composer, and arranger Kenny Kirkland, who played often with Wynton and Branford Marsalis, Sting, Jerry Gonzalez and the Fort Apache Band, and Art Blakey, among many others. Although identified as an African-American, Kenny was equally proud of his Latino heritage. His mother was Puerto Rican. This poem was inspired by a conversation with Kenny regarding race and ethnicity, or what it meant to be black and Puerto Rican on a night when our "artistic family" from both sides of our racial and ethnic spectrum gathered to celebrate the wedding anniversary of a mutual friend, Orlando Godoy.

Easy-flowing river—An indigenous reference for the Hudson River.

Garrison—A street in the Hunts Point neighborhood of the South Bronx.

Ife-A Yoruba deity. Depending on the source one reads, Ife is a deity referring to or linked to the deities of river (or sea, ocean, big body of water). In the African Diaspora, it is linked to Olokun. According to one researcher at http://www.edofolks.com, Olokun was (is) male, but then the deity got transplanted to Ife (female) by Ekaladerhan and subsequently by Cuban Yoruba Lucumi language during the middle period. Within the context of the poem Ife is female and thus the phrase eludes to her elliptical presence inspiring Cuban dance ritual of los Diablitos at this museum exhibition.

Jerry—Trumpeter and percussionist Jerry Gonzalez, leader of the Fort Apache Band.

Joyuda—A coastal town and ward of Cabo Rojo, Puerto Rico located along the southwest coast of Puerto Rico.

La Garita—A barrio and ward of the city and province of Cabo Rojo, Puerto Rico located in the Southwest coast of the island. The word is Spanish for sentry post. Historically, indigenous people, and later pirates and Spaniards, posted lookouts on the high point of this hill to observe the Caribbean Sea for approaching ships.

Glossary of Terms   61

Lares—A town in the central mountains of Puerto Rico. The town is significant in Puerto Rican history, specifically in the rebellion of 1868 against Spain lead by abolitionist, writer, and doctor Dr. Ramon Emeterio Betances.

Laviera—A reference to Puerto Rican poet Tato Laviera.

Mama 'buela—In the common Puerto Rican vernacular it is an affectionate term for grandmother. It is also the title and refrain of a composition written by Puerto Rican percussionist, bandleader and composer, Mr. Tito Puente.

Mani—A ward of the city and province of Mayaguez, Puerto Rico. Mayaguez is located in the west coast region of Puerto Rico.

Mario Rivera—Saxophonist, composer, arranger, and alumnus of most post-World War II-era jazz and Afro-Cuban bands. Among them Machito, Chick Webb, Tito Rodriguez, Tito Puente, Duke Ellington, and Chico O'Farrell, among other. He currently plays for the Lincoln Center Afro-Cuban Jazz Orchestra.

Olú—A spiritual or cosmic deity. It was also a character created by poet Tato Laviera.

Old San Juan—A topless bar in the Hunts Point neighborhood of the South Bronx.

Pandera—A musical instrument similar to the tambourine, only larger.

Parisian Thoroughfare—Composition written by Bud Powell. Bud Powell was considered a significant contributor to post swing jazz—he did away with the left hand stride technique and replaced it with left hand chords on an irregular basis. Tragically, in a racial incident during the early 1940s, he was beaten on the head by police. Powell never fully recovered and suffered from bad headaches and mental breakdowns throughout the remainder of his life. Despite this, he recorded some true gems during 1947-1951 for Roost, Blue Note, and Verve, composing such major works as "Dance of the Infidels," "Hallucinations" (also known as "Budo"), "Un Poco Loco," "Bouncing With Bud," and "Tempus Fugit." For a brief biography see: http://music.yahoo.com/ar-261617-bio—Bud-Powell. Also hear The Genius of Bud Powell, Verve, 1950.

Parkchester—A neighborhood in the south east section of the Bronx. It also a name of a cooperative community in the same neighborhood. The cooperative was built by the Metropolitan Life Insurance company.

Quenepas (or queneps)—A tart fruit native to many Caribbean islands.

Sachem—The formal title among the highland nations meaning clan chief or leader.

Sawanakie—The word developed by the local Wappingos tribe for Europeans.

Sixta—The name of author's mother.

Soundview—A neighborhood in the southeast section of the Bronx.

Sucia and Junior—The names of two cats residing in the New Rican Village Cultural Center.

'Tain—The nickname of jazz percussionist Jeff Watts, a close friend of Kenny Kirkland.

Tonality of Atonement—Composed by Kenny Kirkland and arranged and recorded by Charles Fambrough, The Proper Angle, CTI Records, 1991.

Wecquaesgeek—The indigenous Wappingos or Wappinger nation language. It was the name given to the Bronx River. The Wappingo villages were known to have settled east of the Hudson River and along the Bronx River between the Bronx and Tarrytown.

Wampum—Derived from the word *wampumeag*, a belt-like ornament made of small beads and clamshells bartered and used as ornaments by Native Americans. The local, more superior wampum was manufactured using Long Island clams.

The definitions of the following words and/or phrases were researched in the Dictionary of African American Slang. Clarence Major, editor. Penguin Books. 1971.

Juice back—Drink liquor.

Jumping salty—to get angry.

Knobs—knees.

lay iron on ground—This phrase refers to the act of dancing.

Main drag of many tears—Reference to 125th Street.

Rigor mortis—To be in a bad urban situation, such as unemployed.

Sender—A poet.

Stiffing the Stroll—To be standing on the corner.

Wheelchair—A reference to a car.

Artistic Biography

Américo Casiano Jr. is one of the original Nuyorican poets and a key founding activist for the Nuyorican art movement. He has promoted, produced and coordinated numerous readings and performance series at key arts and cultural organizations in New York City, among them, The Puerto Rican Workshop, Inc., El Museo Del Barrio, Inc., New Rican Village, Inc. the Bronx Council on the Arts and the Metropolitan Literary Program, Inc. He is the recipient of two literary awards: 2003 New York Foundation for the Arts Poetry Fellow and 1974 CAPS Poetry Fellow. His publications include:

Anthologies: T. Medina et al. *Bum Rush The Page: Def Poetry Jam.* New York: Crown Publications. 2001.

G. Johnston et al. *New Rains Volume Nine: Our Fathers/Ourselves.* New York: Blind Beggar Press. 1999.

M. Algarin et al. *Aloud: Voices from the Nuyorican Poets' Café.* New York: Holt/Owl Books. 1994.

J. Bruchac III. *The Next World: Poems by Third World Americans.* Trumansburg: Crossing Press. 1976.

M. Algarin et al. *Nuyorican Poetry.* New York: Wm. Morrow. 1976.

Literary Journals: *Brujala Compass, Panorama, Greenfield Review, Grub Street, New Rains, Revista Del Instituto De Estudios Puertorriqueño De Brooklyn College, Sombra, Latin NY, among others.*

Performances: Américo Casiano Jr. is the founder and artistic director of NuyoRican School Original Poetry Jazz Ensemble, Inc. The ensemble blends the use of the written verse with contemporary jazz/Latin jazz. It maintains two distinct versions: a traveling theatre ensemble and a performance concert ensemble lead by Américo Casiano. Among the concert ensemble's past performers were poets Tato Laviera, Wanda

Ortiz, Maria Aponte and Louis Reyes Rivera. Past musicians have included Arturo O'Farrill, Andy Gonzalez, Phoenix Rivera, Edy Martinez, Ray Martinez, Gene Golden, Milton Cardona, Edgardo Miranda, among others. The concert ensemble has performed in the following venues:

Acentos Poetry Series 2007, Hostos Center for Arts and Culture 2007, Bronx First Wednesday Cultural Trolley 2007, Julia De Burgos Latino Cultural Center 2006, Bronx First Wednesday Cultural Trolley 2006, Bronx Community College Summer Arts Festival 2005, Boricua College, Brooklyn Campus 2006, 2005, 2004, 2003, Aaron Davis Center for the Performing Arts 2003, 2003 GrammyFest, The Jay Liveson Memorial Poetry and Music Festival at the College of Mount Saint Vincent. 2002, Nuyorican Poets' Café. 2003, 2002, 2001, The Golden Ball Festival at Bronx River Arts Center and Gallery. 2001, Ithaca Community School for Music and Art. 2001, and Hostos Center for Arts & Culture 2001.

Visit our web site: www.nuyoricanschool.org.
For bookings call 718-601-1163 ext. 3
Or email: info@nuyoricanschool.org or poetacasiano@yahoo.com.

978-0-595-43289-9
0-595-43289-1

Printed in the United States
108446LV00004B/253-300/A